Joking Around

Funny Families

Chuck Whelon

WINDMILL BOOKS

Published in 2019 by Windmill Books,
an Imprint of Rosen Publishing
29 East 21st Street, New York, NY 10010

Copyright © Arcturus Holdings Ltd, 2019

Editors: Samantha Hilton and Joe Harris, with Julia Adams
Book Design: Stefan Holiland, with Emma Randall

Photo Credits:

Key: b-bottom, t-top, c-center, l-left, r-right
Chuck Wheldon: cover, 1, 3bl, 44b, 5tr, 6bl, 7tr, 8bl, 9tl, 10tl, 11b, 12bl, 13cr, 13bl, 14tl, 15bc, 16br, 17bl, 18tl, 19tr20br, 21b, 22bl, 23tr, 24b; Shutterstock/Memo Angeles: 3tl, 4cl, 5bc, 6tc, 7bc, 8tr, 9bc, 10bl, 11cr, 12tl, 14bl, 15tr, 16tl, 17tc, 18br, 19bl, 20c, 21tc, 22tr, 23bl, 24tr, 25tr, 25bl, 26tl, 26bl, 27tl, 27bc, 28tc, 28br, 29tr, 29bl.

Cataloging-in-Publication Data

Names: Whelon, Chuck.
Title: Funny families / Chuck Whelon.
Description: New York : Windmill Books, 2019. | Series: Joking around
Identifiers: LCCN ISBN 9781508195603 (pbk.) | ISBN 9781508195597 (library bound) | ISBN 9781508195610 (6 pack)
Subjects: LCSH: Families—Juvenile humor.Friendship—Juvenile humor.
Classification: LCC PN6231.F3 W48 2019 | DDC 818'.60208—dc23

Manufactured in the United States of America

CPSIA Compliance Information: Batch #BS18WM: For Further Information contact Rosen Publishing, New York, New York at 1-800-237-9932

Why was the octopus worried about her son?

Because he was a crazy, mixed-up squid!

Did you hear that Uncle Bob lost his wig on the roller coaster?

It was a hair-raising experience!

Riddle me this! I'm tall when I'm young but short when I'm old. What am I?

A candle.

Kurt: What has four legs, pimples, and smells bad?

Bert: Me and my brother!

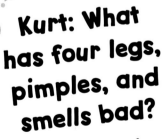

What did the mother dog say to the puppy?

"We're having dinner soon ... don't eat too much homework!"

Why did the woman go out of the house with her purse open?

She expected some change in the weather!

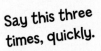

Riddle me this!

What goes up but never comes down?

Your age.

Emily: Dad, I got an A in spelling!

Dad: Don't be silly, there isn't an "A" in "spelling"!

Say this three times, quickly.

Simon's sister's socks sat in a sink soaking in soapsuds!

Raquel: Why does your dad wear two sweaters when he plays golf?

Michelle: In case he gets a hole in one!

What do you get if you cross baked beans with onions?

Tear gas!

What do you get if you cross Dad's socks with a boomerang?

A nasty smell that keeps coming back!

What did the mother broom say to her son at bedtime?

"It's time to go to sweep!"

Knock, knock.

Who's there?

Anita.

Anita who?

Anita borrow a cup of sugar!

What do you do if you find a dinosaur in your bed?

Find somewhere else to sleep!

Why was the little iceberg just like his dad?

Because he was a chip off the cold block!

Knock, knock.
Who's there?
Dishes
Dishes who?
Dish-es me, who are you?

Which fruit do twins like best?

Pears!

What can you give and keep at the same time?

A cold!

Winnie: Why is there a plane outside your bedroom door?

Vinnie: I must have left the landing light on!

My cousin is so silly, he took his computer to the nurse because it had a virus!

Say this three times, quickly.

If your dog chews shoes, whose shoes does he choose?

David's father has three sons: Snap, Crackle, and...?

David!

Why did the boy throw butter out of the window?

To see the butterfly!

Why is your sister so good at sports?

She has athlete's foot!

Say this three times, quickly.

There's a kitten in mittens eating chicken in the kitchen!

Why were the glowworms' parents so happy?

Because their children were all very bright!

Dad: There's a burglar downstairs eating the cake Aunt Agatha baked.

Daughter: Should I call the police or an ambulance?

What is stranger than seeing a cat fish?

Seeing a goldfish bowl!

Kid: Can I have a canary for Christmas?

Dad: No, you'll have turkey, like everyone else!

Daughter: I can't mow the lawn today. I've twisted my ankle.

Mother: That's a lame excuse!

Why was the youngest of seven children late for school?

Because the alarm was set for six!

Knock, knock.

Who's there?

Aunt.

Aunt who?

Aunt you gonna let me in?

Why did the cat always hang out near the piano?

She was looking for the piano tuna!

What should you do if a teenage monster rolls her eyes at you?

Roll them back to her!

Knock, knock.

Who's there?

Someone on a pogo stick.

Tell them to hop off!

Say this three times, quickly.

Will merry Murray marry Mary or Marie?

When should
a mouse stay
indoors?

When it's raining
cats and dogs!

What do you
give to a baby
snake?

A rattle!

I am a room
with no walls.
What am I?

A mushroom.

Why shouldn't you
worry if you see mice
in your home?

They're probably
doing the
mouse-work!

What do you
say to someone
sitting on
your roof?

"High there!"

Say this three times, quickly.

I like a proper cup of coffee from a proper copper coffeepot!

"Son, why didn't you come straight home from school?"

"Because we live around the corner!"

Son: This fish has bones in it.

Mother: Are you choking?

Son: No, I'm serious!

What did the Italian say when he returned from an overseas trip?

"Rome, sweet Rome!"

Sean: Why does your dog wear gloves?

Vaughn: It's a boxer!

"My dad had to go to court for stealing a calendar. You know what he got?"

"Twelve months!"

What ancient land is like your brother's bedroom?

Mess-opotamia!

Why are there more ghost cats than ghost dogs?

Because every cat has nine lives!

"Why is your brother running around his bed?"

"He's trying to catch up on his sleep!"

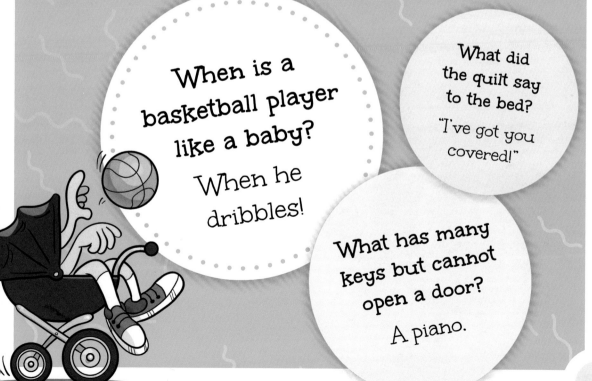

When is a basketball player like a baby?

When he dribbles!

What did the quilt say to the bed?

"I've got you covered!"

What has many keys but cannot open a door?

A piano.

Thelma: If that planet is Mars, what's the one higher up?
Velma: Is it Pa's?

What happened when the invisible man married the invisible woman?
Their kids were nothing to look at!

Who are small, furry, and fantastic at sword fighting?
The Three Mouseketeers!

What happened when Granny Smith married Mr. Braeburn?
They lived appley ever after!

Why are you eating that baguette in the bathtub?

It's a sub sandwich!

Knock, knock.

Who's there?

Little old lady.

Little old lady who?

Wow! I didn't know you could yodel!

What prize did the inventor of the door knocker win?

The No-bell Prize!

What instrument do dogs like best?

The trom-bone!

Edwin: I don't like cheese with holes.

Dad: Well, eat the cheese, and leave the holes on the side of your plate!

How do you know when there's an elephant under your bed?

Your nose is touching the ceiling!

Knock, knock.

Who's there?

Amit.

Amit who?

Amit your sister at the movies last night!

Riddle me this!

What belongs to you, even though other people use it more than you do?

Your name.

How do you make antifreeze?

Hide her coat and gloves!

Teacher: What is the plural of baby?

Frances: Twins!

What do a pet dog and a phone have in common?

They both have collar I.D.!

Say this three times, quickly.

These tricky tongue twisters trip thrillingly off the tongue!

Why do dogs run in circles?

Because it's hard to run in squares!

Why did the police officer arrest his cat?

He saw the kitty litter!

What did the mother cow say to her calf at night?

"It's pasture bedtime!"

I go up and down but never move. What am I?

Stairs.

Why did the jogger eat on the run?

She loved fast food!

Why was the baby panda so spoiled?

Because its mother panda-d to its every whim!

Riddle me this!
What goes up when the rain comes down?
An umbrella.

Why are an old man's teeth like stars?
Because they come out at night!

Why is the letter "A" most like a flower?
Because the "B" is after it!

Why was the cat silent?
A person got its tongue!

How do you know carrots are good for your eyes?
Because you never see a rabbit wearing glasses!

Dan: My teacher says I should train to be an astronaut.

Anne: No, he said you're a real space cadet!

Which relative visits astronauts in outer space?

Auntie Gravity!

Why was 6 scared of 7?

Because 7, 8, 9!

What does a fashionable house wear?

Address!

Spike: My dog's got no nose!

Mike: How does he smell?

Spike: Terrible!

Why did the mushroom get invited to so many parties?

Because he was a fun guy!

Little pencil: You look as though you've put on weight, Dad.

Daddy pencil: You're very blunt!

What makes you say your brother is silly?

He tried to borrow Facebook from the library!

What time is it when an elephant sits on your fence?

Time to get a new fence!

Riddle me this!
I have one foot, one head, and four legs. What am I?
A bed.

Knock, Knock.
Who's there?
Cash.
Cash who?
I knew you were a nut!

Did you hear about the magician who tried his sawing-a-person-in-two tricks at home?
He had lots of half brothers and sisters!

My dad can juggle eggshells, yesterday's newspaper, and an empty box!
That's garbage!

Mother: Please can you help me fix dinner?

Daughter: Why, is it broken?

Dad: Why have you been missing school, son?

Son: I haven't missed it one little bit!

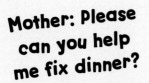

How do you define "cartoon"?

Music you listen to in the car!

What do you call cheese that isn't yours?

Nacho cheese!

Do robots have brothers?

No, but they do have transistors!

What do you call a baby skunk?

A little squirt!

What did the baby corn say to his mother?

Where's Pop?

Knock, knock.

Who's there?

Lettuce.

Lettuce who?

Lettuce in! We're freezing!

My mother's excellent at history, but she's an awful cook.

She's an expert on ancient grease!

Did you hear about the embarrassing dads in the fathers' race? One ran in short bursts, the other ran in burst shorts!

"Did your mother help you with your homework?"

"No, I got it wrong all by myself!"

I am as light as a feather, but no one can hold me for long. What am I?

Your breath.

Why did the programmer sell his cat?

He thought it might eat his mouse!

Why did the students eat their homework? Because the teacher said that it was a piece of cake!

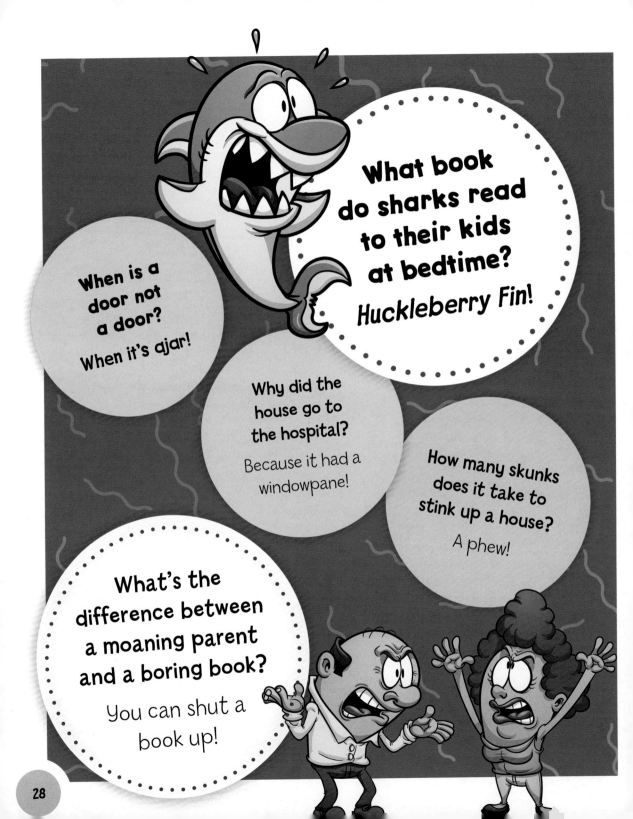

What kind of monster lives in your brother's room?

The Loch Mess Monster!

How do you warm up a room after it's been painted?

Give it a second coat!

Annie: Why did your dad quit his job at the can-crushing plant?"

Danny: Because it was soda pressing!

Did you hear about the cat that swallowed a ball of yarn?

She had mittens!

Glossary

athlete's foot An infection of the foot.

boomerang A curved object. When thrown in a certain way, it flies in a big curve, eventually returning to the thrower.

Braeburn A kind of apple.

canary A species of bird that is yellow, and often kept as a pet.

cashew A kind of nut.

chip A small piece of something that has been removed from a much larger object, often in the process of chopping, cutting, or breaking.

decay The process of something organic rotting.

down A type of feather used in pillows.

dribble To have saliva running from one's mouth; in basketball, to run with the ball while bouncing it off the floor.

fungi Living organisms that produce spores, such as mushrooms.

Granny Smith A kind of apple.

nachos A dish of tortilla chips, topped with cheese and other savory foods.

pasture Grass-covered land on which cattle graze.

pirate Something that has been produced and/or sold illegally.

programmer A person who writes code for computers.

ratatouille A vegetarian dish.

skunk A black and white animal that sprays a strong-smelling liquid when defending itself.

soapsuds Froth made of soap and water.

sub A type of sandwich that consists of a baguette-shaped roll cut open and filled with cheese, cold meats, vegetables, and condiments.

transistor A tiny device that controls the flow of electricity.

Further Information

Books:

Dahl, Michael. *The Everything Kids' Giant Book of Jokes, Riddles, and Brain Teasers*. London, UK: Adams Media, 2010.

Kingfisher. *A Joke A Day: 365 Guaranteed Giggles* (Sidesplitters). London, UK: Kingfisher, 2007.

MacIntyre, Mickey. *The Really Funny Knock! Knock! Joke Book for Kids*. Inverness, UK: Bell & Mackenzie Publishing, 2014.

Regan, Lisa. *The Big Book of Riddles*. London, UK: Arcturus, 2014.

Rosen, Michael. *The Laugh Out Loud Joke Book*. London, UK: Scholastic, 2016.

For web resources related to the subject of this book, go to: www.windmillbooks.com/weblinks and select this book's title.

Index